THE TRUTH ABOUT WHITE PEOPLE

Essays for and about white people
in these United States of America

LOLA E. PETERS

First Edition
ISBN: 9780989865838-0-0

This book is dedicated to all the people of color who continue to survive the daily assaults of racism. We are the manifested dreams of our ancestors. What power they have put into creating our very bones! What a privilege to walk the path they dreamt into being and what a breathtaking responsibility to create the path for the generations to come. How honored I am to walk alongside you all.

ACKNOWLEDGEMENTS

Special thanks to Mr. Omar Willey for his expert review and light editorial touch on this book. Never doubt.

Table of Contents

INTRODUCTION

While I worked for Macy's, a son of one of my colleagues joined the Army and was sent to Iraq. Before his deployment, I would have described her as one of the most serene, grounded people I knew. Day by day, I watched her change. She began to drink more. She was tense. Her judgment on major events began to deteriorate. Her friendships shifted. Normally a kind-hearted, thoughtful person, a mean cattiness emerged in her.

In a conversation a few months after her son returned from his final deployment, she spoke about feeling like she had awoken from a very bad dream. She said she had suddenly become aware of how tensely she had been holding her body during his deployments, how fear had attached itself to her at a cellular level. I saw her laugh freely again that day for the first time since he had left.

This is a familiar story and experience to families of military veterans. It is also the story of every black parent.

A black Facebook® friend recently posted about learning that his adolescent son had been playing in a nearby park when a shooting occurred. He expressed relief that his son had left the playground unhurt. For a black parent, this type of incident carries multiple fears: will their child accidentally be killed in a public incident; when the police arrive, if they arrive, will their child be subjected to harassment and additional danger; how can they maintain their child's self-respect and sense of agency in the world in the face of constant pressure from all sides.

Since Trayvon Martin's murder in February of 2012, white Americans have been faced with the unassailable evidence that black Americans are treated differently by law enforcement. This has led to dialog about all of the other social, political, religious, cultural, and economic arenas where people of color face aggression and hostility.

Yet the response to these events remains the same: if only black people would [fill in the blank], these awful things wouldn't happen to them. Even our first black president, in response to the police murder of a string of innocent, young black men, created a commission to fix young black men.

The truth: **there is nothing wrong with young black men that isn't also wrong with young white men**. The differences arise in how systems and institutions treat them, treat all black people and people of color. I believe it's time to stop trying to fix people of color, especially black people, and time to face squarely how white people's mythology and self-seduction about their superiority damage us all.

I began writing this series of essays as Facebook® posts after Michael Brown was murdered in Ferguson, Missouri in the summer of 2014. Each essay uses my personal experiences to examine the difference between the myths of white superiority and the truth of how whiteness is expressed in various aspects of our national culture.

These essays provide a basis for debate and dialogue about whiteness. By publishing the stories and the essays, I hope to encourage other people of color to come forward with their own stories. We need to stop protecting white people from the consequences of the racism designed for their prosperity and success.

I also hope white people, especially Millenials, will recognize the need to change their own paradigm and liberate themselves from the destructive legacy of whiteness and use the stories and essays in this book to examine how they perpetuate racism. Then I hope they will join people of color in the very hard work of dismantling the structures that perpetuate it.

1. THE BASICS

I know white people. Oh, yes, I know lots of individual white people. But more important, certainly for this series of essays, I know well that collection of human beings known as "white people." I've studied them all my life, the same way Jane Goodall has studied chimpanzees. Like her, I've often travelled invisibly among and beside my subjects as a perceived non-threatening, presence. My skin tone doesn't immediately reveal my racial identity. This allows me to move among white people not as an "other" but rather as one of them. I see, unfiltered, their work habits, family structures and functions. I see their social norms and cultural adaptations. I have had white friends, family members, and lovers all my life, even a white ex-husband. I see white people.

I was raised in the 1950s and '60s in a Northern California town; population 10,000, of which twenty-five of us were "Negro," with only my younger brother near my age. Since he was three years behind me in school, I was always the black kid in my grade (as was he in his).

Over the years I've travelled extensively throughout the US for personal and professional reasons. I've lived in California, Nevada, Washington, Texas, Pennsylvania, and Massachusetts.

From 1967 to 1990 I worked for several large corporations and government agencies. Whether the company employed three or three thousand, I was always the only black professional. After 1990, the number of African American peers picked up a bit, as two or three other black professionals sometimes joined me in the workplace. Before then, however, I saw at most one or two support staff: file clerks, secretaries, or janitors.

In every job before 1990, I started out as a contract employee and then proved myself too valuable to let go. Other black applicants for jobs in those organizations were turned away from professional opportunities, while white applicants with limited knowledge, skill, or experience were hired. I was frequently put in the position of training white employees with less knowledge, skill, and experience who were then promoted over me. I was even once told "We only promote people who look like our customers, and we don't have customers who look like you."

All of these experiences have allowed me to observe and learn the inner workings of whiteness. This book combines my experiences and reflections on those inner workings. Let's begin by setting out some basics.

The vast majority of white people think that black people deserve whatever it is that happens to us. They think the bad things are the result of our own choices and actions. While they occasionally feel sorry for how things turn out for us, they believe it's our own fault.

When white people read that our young men are arrested more often than white young men they believe it's because we commit more crime. When they read that our high school graduation rates are lower than theirs they assume that it's because we don't value education. When they see that our unemployment rates are high, they assume it's because we're lazy, or living off welfare, or aren't trying hard enough. Seldom do they care about the consistently contrary actual findings of gazillions of research studies or even our own true-life experiences.

At first I believed in the kind of thinking embodied by Maya Angelou's statement that "when you know better, you do better." I believed that white people simply didn't know better. But years of observation have changed that belief. For example, a simple Google search using "crime rates by race" will return a page full of independent reports showing that most crimes are committed by white men, that sentencing for the same crimes are disproportionately more severe for men of color. White people know this. They really do understand that we are as capable as they are collectively. They really do know that we have gone to the highest court in the country to get access to quality education. They really do know that domestic abuse is rampant in their own midst; that abuse of drugs is prevalent among their own teens; that white women are more likely to be raped by a white man than a black one. Still, they cling to the myths.

Why? Because these myths allow them to never question their own worthiness. Like the aging diva, convinced she's not getting the good parts because younger women are sleeping with the right people, and not asking whether her skills have faded, these myths allow them to believe that they are, personally and collectively, actually superior. They can then delude themselves into believing that their "hard work" got them whatever societal perks they have, that working an eight-hour day reading spreadsheets for $25-$50/hour to make a mortgage payment is harder than working construction during the day for $15/hour and then cleaning office buildings at a second night job for $8/hour to pay rent. They can convince themselves they have "made it" on their own without seeing the ladder built by generations of opportunities given their parents and grandparents, whether on this continent or another.

This mass delusion comes with a cost, one that often plays out as life and death.

If you've seen Alex Garland's video showing the pepper-spraying of Raymond Wilford by a Westlake Mall security guard in Seattle, you know that the actual person causing the disturbance was a white man. Garland's still photos show that moments before, one white man grabbed another white man by the collar and had to be physically subdued and separated from the altercation by other white men. This same first white man, who became known as the "shirtless white man," then confronted several others including one young black man and then the second young black man who the security guard pepper-sprayed. The photo sequence shows that the guard was on scene before the altercation between the shirtless man and the young black man.

As the security guard is pepper-spraying the young black man, the shirtless white man walks away. When the police officer arrives, the shirtless white man is gone from view. The guard's racist profiling of a young black man has allowed a violent, aggressive, perhaps dangerous, white man to walk free; a man who has shown no fear, even of other white men. If this man commits a murder the next day his defense attorney might be able to say in court that he has no prior criminal record. Unlike the young black man, he will be presumed innocent until proven guilty. And the security guard? Even if he's fired by his current employer, he can move on to another job where his profiling can continue because no employer will ask whether he has ever been involved in profiling an innocent man.

These actions put everyone who shops at Westlake Mall at risk: the young black man who was just meeting up with a friend to shop at the mall; the white shopper who innocently comes across a crazed, shirtless, white man; the white protesters who had their constitutional right to peacefully gather shattered; the young, white women who kept screaming that the guard had the wrong man and learned that their racial power is instantly diminished when they side with a man of color.

Who knows what the shirtless man will do next, whom he will harm? Like Timothy McVeigh and James Holmes before him, his white skin has protected him from suspicion. It has endangered all of the rest of us. This is the shadow side of white presumptions of their superiority.

This series of essays explores how the mythology of white superiority damages us all and how the social, political, ethical structure of our country that has been built upon it cannot survive.

2. RACISM IN THE WORKPLACE

Let's start with some stories from my own experience. To stay focused on my beloved Seattle, I'll just use recent examples, from my Bon Marché/ Macy's years (1998-2008).

Story #1: Somehow I got hornswoggled into joining the Diversity Committee. Perhaps it was because of my prior employment as Director for Antiracism & Justice Programs for a national non-profit. {Note to my POC friends: run like hell from these jobs/opportunities, white people do}. Anyway, back to the story. It's 1999ish and the committee has a very intense meeting where the Senior VP for Human Resources tells us all about how very committed he is to diversifying the staff, especially at the management level. This man has been in his job for at least five years, and came from a similar high-level position elsewhere. He spoke passionately about his personal history with diversity and how he grew up in South Boston during desegregation of their schools (not a hopeful note, by the way). After about a half hour of this deeply sincere speech, he said he would hire a person of color as a manager in a heartbeat, if only he could find someone who had the qualifications, experience, and the right attitude.

OK, POC, breathe. We're not done.

While this type of statement sets all POC on fire, to white people it seems like a perfectly appropriate set of guidelines. Why? Because that's how they believe they've gotten their jobs and promotions. Except…except I knew that the white man who was then Senior VP of my department had a habit of walking into rooms and screaming at people, going as far as calling them names and throwing tantrums. I also knew that he, a married man, was having an affair with a woman in another department and had just fired his assistant, with whom he was also having an affair. Nearly everyone in the company knew. No… I'm not kidding.

So, I went on a mission. I took a poll of people in several departments and asked three questions: (1) Do you know anyone who became a manager in this organization before they had the full qualifications; (2) Do you know anyone who became a manager in this organization who didn't have the requisite management experience when they were hired; and (3) Do you know any managers who have bad attitudes? The overwhelming response to all three questions was "YES." So, I put my findings in an email to said Senior VP of Human Resources with a cc: to the entire

Diversity Committee and asked, based on my findings, if there was a separate standard and set of prerequisites being established for people of color to become managers, and whether that difference didn't perpetuate discrimination. He and his staff were clearly violating the very standards he demanded of people of color.

The lesson: white people are so surrounded by discriminatory practice in their favor that they're like fish in water. The majority of them don't even realize there is a question to ask, let alone what the question is. If a "trusted person" makes a statement, they just believe it, especially if it's delivered with emotion. This is why critical thinking isn't encouraged in our schools. Instead our advertising culture says "See that pretty face, how can you question what they say?" It's this inability and unwillingness to think critically that reinforces white people's belief in their innate goodness and superiority.

Colleagues in my department were living under the thumb of a tyrannical bully, and it took another couple of years and the intervention of outsiders to get rid of him. When he finally left, the change in my coworkers, the sense of liberation, was palpable. There were, of course, a small number who had benefitted from his tyranny, and they manifested their own bullying tendencies by undermining other co-workers and doing their best to sow dissent through gossip and innuendo. Eventually they, too, were pushed out of the organization.

Saddest of all, though, this bully had been in the company's management for at least a decade. They had passed up qualified, committed staff members for this guy, and had institutionalized a system that ensured they would continue to get the same low quality of manager. Yet when asked why there were no managers who were people of color, especially African American, the institution fell back on an ideal they didn't expect of white employees.

None of the white people on the committee questioned the standards. Those criteria for management selection sounded right to them. They never asked if those standards reflected the reality they lived in. Asking that question would have led them to an analysis of the organization's internal processes and provided them with data on which they could have built their own liberation from tyranny. This is one example of how when #BlackLivesMatter it can impact everyone.

Story #2: I worked with a brilliant programmer. He had authored an internal marketing financial management application that was just amazing. I had to work closely with him because the system he designed was the same system I had to support, and create manuals and training for.

We worked in cubicles and there was near constant banter between co-workers. From the first day I began working in the department this programmer refused to speak to me. If I asked him a question, instead of answering me directly, he would turn to someone else nearby and answer as if he was speaking to them. If no one was around, I got no reply. He wouldn't put any paper directly into my hand, nor would he take paper directly from my hands. I first thought he had Obsessive Compulsive Disorder (OCD), but then I noticed that he only did this with me. Another programmer worked closely with him part-time, and they would often tell sexist jokes or use coded racist language (welfare queens, dropouts, druggies).

I tried a variety of direct approaches to dealing with the situation, but he would have none of it. He simply ignored me, so I went to my supervisor, who told me that he never saw the problem and since I was the newcomer, it was my responsibility to figure out how to make it work or elect to find other employment. The behavior escalated. I went to the Vice President of our department. She told me that the programmer had had a difficult life, gone through a rough divorce, even had to sleep in her basement for several months, and had just recently pulled his life together and married another member of our staff. {Yes, I know...} As politely as I possibly could, suppressing my inner screaming angry black woman, I explained that I had great sympathy for difficult lives, in fact mine had been no picnic, but that I believed {the magic words} that he was creating a hostile working environment for me and that it couldn't continue. I followed up the meeting with a memo detailing the behavior and the steps I had taken to address it.

The magic words automatically escalated the issue to Human Resources (HR). A few days later I was called into a meeting with HR to explain what happened. Then I was told that the programmer wanted to speak with me privately, one-on-one. Clearly seeing the distress on my face, the HR representative said I could opt out of that, but if I wanted to do the meeting with him it would be in a safe space. Because I believe in second chances, I agreed.

Very painfully, he apologized in private. He was not willing to face the "humiliation" of apologizing to me in front of others, despite his willingness to humiliate me publicly. As it turned out, he had married into a family where he instantly gained a black son-in-law who he'd been treating abysmally. His fairly new wife was threatening divorce if he didn't get his act together.

We continued to work together for ten years, always tenuously. I never trusted him. Ever. I respected his work enormously, but never trusted or respected him.

Lesson 1: White people's negation of people of color's experiences (similar to the negation of rape victims' experiences) is a regular thing. They believe that because they don't experience negative behavior from someone, no one else does either. They also believe that any negative behavior must have been triggered by an action that justifies it. All this they hold true despite their knowledge of the historical impact of racism.

My supervisor didn't see what was happening because he and the programmer were buddies. He either refused to believe that the programmer could treat him one way and me completely differently, or he secretly believed the programmer had a right to behave abusively toward me.

Lesson 2: My supervisor's silence and VP's complicity sent the abuser the message that there would be no consequences, so he continued his harassing behavior. In fact, he briefly expanded his harassment to include other people. People who abuse will only expand their abuse when they have established a sense of confidence.

I have lots more of these stories from my Bon/Macy's years. For example, there's the one about the white Senior VP who served on the Board of the Urban League, and sat in the front row at every Martin Luther King Day celebration, but who yanked a catalog out of production at the last minute, because it featured a black model, with the declaration "We will never put a black model on our covers." I had to involve the regional president of the company to resolve that one.

Though we call these "micro-aggressions," they are exhausting, health-destroying, and morally bankrupting experiences. I'm worn out just remembering them.

White people see only what comforts them and reassures them of their place in the world. What power there would be if they simply woke up and realized how much damage racism is doing to them. We are canaries in their coalmine, and we're dying. Do they not know what happens next?

3. CULTURE

Want a really good chuckle? Ask a white person "What's your favorite thing about white culture?" The blank look on their face is absolutely precious. Some will recover after a second or two and say something like "Well, I'm not really into {ballet/classical music/opera}." Or they'll say, "I don't know… what do you mean by white culture?" Some may say, "Well, white people invented everything that's made our country great." Underneath it all is an honest confusion. Only liberals and progressives (and I'll get to them in an essay all their own) might say "There's no such thing." Which is, by the way, not true. There is a real, significant reason for their confusion, and that reason is playing out in our very current era with Latinos. But first let's back up for some basic definitions.

Everybody gets the concepts of race and culture mixed up. That's not an accident. If the lines were clearly defined then the implications would be pretty powerful. Ah, but the lines can be clearly defined. History helps us define them, and here's how it shakes out. Racially, you're either white or you're not. Period. That's all that counts. Oh, sure, the history of race has other racial categories: Negroid, Mongoloid, Australoid and Caucasoid; Caucasian, Mongolian, Ethiopian, American, and Malay, etc. These categories were all invented by theorists from France, England, and Germany. Surprise, surprise, they decided that anyone who looked and acted like them was the standard for perfection and therefore all others were inferior, and they decided to call themselves Caucasian White, for short. The closer another racial category came to matching theirs, the closer to perfection it was deemed to be. To be White was to be stoic, self-controlled. European rules of court (a.k.a. courtesy) were to be the aspirational standards for social behavior. It was possible to be White without achieving those standards, but you had to acknowledge them and aspire to them.

This was no big deal. People have been coming up with stupid theories about existence and one another since the beginning of time. Unfortunately for them, fortunately for most of the world, there often does emerge a true, right, answer that disproves their base theory of superiority. The earth, for example, is not flat. However, we often have gaps in history between the birth of someone's idiotic idea and proof it is actually idiotic. And sometimes, in the gap, the theory becomes the basis for societal policy and action.

The British Empire was magnificent at using the newfangled, repurposed, theoretical categorization by race as the basis for policy and action. They used it to enslave South Asia and much of Africa. They used it to justify the theft of property and resources in Southern Africa, South Asia, and the Americas. As Southern Africa and the Americas became independent of Britain, the British took the lunacy of race to a whole new level.

I distinguished earlier between the English and the British. Because these here United States of America are the place I want to focus on in these essays, I'll keep my comments focused there. It's in this distinction between English and British that we see the divide between race and culture.

By the time the first Irish immigrants came to the U.S., whiteness had been established as the benchmark for access to property. In a capitalist society, property is the basis of all access to power. The Irish were not classified as white and were excluded from jobs, property ownership, and other perks of being white. English society looked down at them as a subjugated people. The immigrant Irish majority was Catholic, and the English (even the English-Americans) remembered the historic divisions. The Irish had strong cultural ties: their own language, music, dance, art, and poetry. Unlike the generally stoic English, the Irish were stereotyped as passionate people. The N-word was even applied to Irish immigrants. In fact, they began to form alliances with people of African descent, and many among the first generations of immigrants were strong supporters of equal rights.

But then along came the second generation. They looked around and saw that power came with being white, and that being white meant giving up their religion, and music, and dance, and poetry, and everything that distinguished them as separate from the ruling English-Americans. It meant becoming aspirational-English. It meant deciding that people of African descent were at the bottom of human development, that Asians were just above that rung in the evolutional ladder, and they would now side with whiteness. And so, in some form or another, they did just that. They bought entry into whiteness by selling their cultural (and perhaps spiritual) souls.

The Irish were not alone in this transition. In fact, Italians, Greeks, Portuguese, Spanish and other subsequent immigrant groups made the same choice. Their skin color gave them the option to become white by walking away from their native culture and boldly going where every other European had gone before.

This is how we got to an absurd place where a term like "classical music" is universally accepted to mean one kind of music and no one asks: classical Chinese; or classical Swiss; or classical Ethiopian; or classical Hawaiian. I mean, really. How patronizing, presumptuous, and condescending is that? History shows that Africa and Asia had classical forms of their music while Europeans were still sitting around the bonfires of the Middle Ages, for pete's sake. (KING-FM, I'm talking to you… I love the music you play… it feeds my soul… but it's just one kind of classical music. Either expand your selection or change the lingo. "Classical European" would work, if that's all you're going to play.)

I digress.

Problems arise not with these idiotic classifications, but rather with their empowerment by fiat. When laws are based on their categorizations, they become embedded in social practice and their impact is multigenerational. I might hate the color purple, but that only becomes a big deal if I have the power to pass and then enforce a law that says anyone wearing the hideous color purple will be shot the following dawn. A few shootings and purple would leave our culture in short order. Likewise, if I said everyone had to wear something green every day, people would soon hate green but they'd wear it. The next generation may never even see the color purple but they would take green for granted and assume it's the appropriate color for everything.

Lucky for us all I don't have that kind of power. But if I convinced enough people that wearing purple causes war, and got a mob up on my side with lots of "evidence," who knows? In our U.S. of A. we have similar presumptions of what constitutes "proper" cultural behavior. And white people freak out when those internalized rules are challenged.

Example 1: A group of black intellectuals is having a conversation about the nature of religion in the world. We listen respectfully to one another until someone says something outrageous, or funny, or controversial. Then we all burst in at once. This is fun. We all hear one another just fine, and if you pay attention you can tell that we're simultaneously listening and responding, because the conversation is not static, it's advancing. We may call each other crazy or ignorant or silly, all with an undertone of affection. None of us are disturbed by the cacophony of multiple voices speaking at once. The conversation may break into dyads or triads, but it will eventually come back to one single conversation and everyone will have heard the gist of all of the mini-dialogues.

In the meantime, white people in the room, especially white women, are clutching the edges of their seats with terror. They have been told the equivalent of "don't wear purple" for many generations. Loud noises in their white culture mean discord that can lead to potential violence. There are a few exceptions to this… Italians and Greeks have been given permission to be loud and rowdy by way of stereotype, but their assimilated whiteness defines this behavior as comic and unthreatening, ethnically cute. Whites perceive multiple conversations as dangerous dissent. Rather than viewing the situation in light of their lack of ability to track multiple conversations, their deficiency, they mark it as a danger and sign of disrespect. That done, they can completely dismiss both the dynamics and substance of the conversation.

Every single black woman I know who is a career professional has these words somewhere in her job performance reviews: "People are intimidated by you." This, of course, is code language for "You scare white women." What it really means is "You don't behave with the timidity and deference we expect from you" (a.k.a. "You don't seem to know your place, which is beneath me. Even if you are further up the professional ladder than I am").

Example 2: I co-founded Poetry+Motion several years ago. As a member of Seattle's African American Writers' Alliance, I was frustrated by the dearth of opportunities for us to present our poetry. While Elliott Bay Books always reserved the 4th Saturday of February for us to present our work in their reading room, we were seldom individually or collectively invited to participate in other readings. Poetry+Motion was founded as a space for African-American poets and dancers to present our creativity and stretch our muscles publicly.

In my capacity as co-founder, I attended a 2011 workshop on grants sponsored by the City of Seattle's Department of Arts & Culture. About 50 other people were in the workshop. Seated in a very large circle, we each introduced ourselves by giving our name, organization, and the type of work we did. I introduced myself and explained that our organization brought together local African American dancers and poets in a unique collaboration to present original work. As I finished my sentence, a white woman (around my age) yelled from across the room: "You mean spoken word." No, in fact I didn't. There were plenty of places for spoken word poets to perform. But there are many African American poets, like me, who don't use that particular form of poetic expression. We write haiku, couplets, free verse, Tanka and many other types of poetry. I, for one, *wish* I had the skill to write and perform spoken word, but that isn't among my chosen forms. Apparently this woman's reading list didn't include the work of Poet Lauriat Lucile Clifton. Or Audre Lorde. Or Maya Angelou. Or Toni Giovanni. Or Langston Hughes. Or Robert Johnson. Or Amiri Baraka. Or Georgia McDade. Or Santiago Vega.

Sadly, this woman probably felt really proud of herself, that she knew something about black culture. What she proved, though, was that she knew nothing about the complexity of black culture. AND she presumptuously, arrogantly, patronizingly, and condescendingly thought she had the right to correct me about my own culture. I wish I could tell you this is the only time this kind of thing has happened to me, but not even.

White people have given up their own historic cultural roots in order to become aspirationally white. They starve for something real and often glom on to other cultures for sustenance. They adopt African garb, profess religions they have no rooted understanding of, and even marry into other cultures to create an identity for themselves. I've worked among these people and the loneliness they exude breaks my heart.

This cultural dissociation leads to a lack of empathy allowing them to justify the murder of an innocent child. The number of white women who have called or emailed me during the year since Trayvon Martin was killed to ask what they should do stuns me. If it were their own child that had been murdered, or their nephew, or neighbor, what would they do? Why do they need me to tell them what to do?

This same distancing from their own culture permits them to gleefully perform something as grotesque as The Mikado. Ask a group of white women how they would feel if men dressed up as women and then played the exaggerated part of submissive, over-emotional, incompetents. While they would find that offensive, they struggle to empathetically connect with its parallel in race.

This same separation from their hearts allows them to take their children to a picnic at the foot of a lynched man or to see a dead child lying in the street for four hours without screaming for preservation of his dignity. It allows them to put handcuffs on a seven-year-old child who fought with a classmate. It allows them to celebrate the execution of a man with the mental capacity of a young child.

My hope for the millennial generation of whites is that they will see that the whiteness of their parents and grandparents came at a cost. The benefits are the cars, houses, boats, and all the rest. The cost is the distance from their humanity. The impact is felt around the world by war, economic imperialism, and environmental destruction.

4. More Culture

Well, I thought I was done with the cultural aspects, but the topic keeps itching, so I must scratch. And apparently I'm not done with Macy's stories, either, so here we go.

I will never forget my first day of third grade. See, I was born in Ethiopia (African American father, Ethiopian-Greek mother). After leaving Ethiopia, my family lived for a few months with my father's sister in Berkeley, California. Eight months later we moved to a small suburb twenty miles south; a 99.9% all-white suburb. Because my prior education, through second grade, had been in a Catholic-run missionary school in Ethiopia, I had to take an IQ test to determine my grade level. I scored at a sixth grade level in every subject. Because I had already skipped a grade in Ethiopia, my parents naively decided it would be best for my socialization if I entered my new school in the third grade.

So, here it was, my first day of third grade. Although there had been significant controversy about my existence already, and the kids knew I had come from *Africa*, the teacher formally called me to the front of the classroom and introduced me to the class. Misinterpreting my family history, she introduced me as the daughter of an Ethiopian princess and told all that I had scored the highest IQ in the district's history. After her few words of introduction she asked the class if anyone had questions for me.

The first question left me utterly confused: how did I like wearing clothes? Now, understand, my family in Ethiopia had a dressmaker who made all of our clothes. Occasionally my great aunt in Galveston would send clothes, but most of the clothing we wore was specially made for us, often using fashion from England and France as patterns. I had worn clothes all my life. Everyone I had ever known wore clothes. All the kids I had gone to school with wore clothes, even though they came from a wide range of economic backgrounds. Everyone I had seen my entire life, everywhere I went, wore clothes. I had never been exposed to the movies made in the U.S. depicting Africans as naked savages, and had absolutely no idea what this question meant.

The second question was equally confusing: how did I like living indoors? I had lived indoors all my life. The home we left in Ethiopia was a three-bedroom house with a foyer, large living room, and a dining room that could comfortably seat 16 for dinner. The furniture was all hand made in Italy. The front yard contained a circular driveway inside of which was a garden of various types of flowers. We had a cook and a gardener. My brother and I each had nannies. A large, stone, wall surrounded the property, and a little corner store was built into one part of the wall. I knew many people who lived in traditional Ethiopian thatched homes, and many who lived in homes like ours, but no one who lived outdoors.

Forty years later I went to work for Macy's. Surely things would have changed! Surely the advances in travel and technology would have changed people's knowledge and perception of the world. Oh, if only.

A white woman I worked with at Macy's had been born in Mozambique to white, U.S., missionary parents while Mozambique was still a Portuguese colony. The family returned to the States when she was nine and had never gone back to Mozambique. In fact, the woman had never again left the Pacific Northwest, not even to vacation in other parts of the country. It was now the late 1990s. She was in her 30s and had an opportunity to go back to Mozambique with her parents and husband for an extended trip. Since she didn't have enough vacation time, she quit her Macy's job and joined the family on their journey.

After they returned, she came back to visit the office occasionally. Someone suggested she do a slide presentation about her trip and a brown-bag lunchtime presentation was scheduled in one of the department's conference rooms.

I vacillated over attending. Because my family had a relationship with the Ethiopian royal family, we often hosted events for people from the States who came to visit. This was a bit tricky, since it was the 1950s and rabid racism was quite alive and well in the U.S. of A. Most white U.S. government representatives who came to Ethiopia accepted my parents' participation in royal-sponsored events, and visiting people of color nearly always became an extension of our family. But white private citizens were iffy, seldom willing to cross the lines of racial taboos unless there was a major boost to their economic or social status as a payoff.

As for missionaries, they fell into three categories: (1) those who genuinely interacted with people at every level and in every sector of Ethiopian life; (2) those who lived in gated, locked compounds, interacted with high-status Ethiopians, and only interacted with the local population in formal, structured ways (as preachers, teachers and the like); and (3) those who interacted only with other white people and, when necessary, the Ethiopian elite. All three categories sent letters home to their constituents telling about the amazing work they were doing converting people to Christianity. Their letters always featured a raggedy looking child and implied that the missionary had saved this child from some horrible fate or the other by converting them, or could do so if only they had a few more dollars. This was particularly amusing since Ethiopia's primary religion has been Christianity since the 1st century AD, just after the religion was founded. A small Muslim population developed over time, but Christianity still dominates the country.

A case to make my point. In the 1960s, my family was living in a suburb about 20 miles south of Oakland, CA. My father received word that a very important white missionary was coming to a nearby church to talk about the tremendously important work he was doing in Ethiopia and how successful it was. My parents knew the man, and knew he belonged to the category of missionary that only interacted with other white people. Relishing the results, our family went to the event and sat in a pew near the back of the church. The missionary was to speak after the collection was taken. Instead of money, my father put his business card in the collection plate, which was then taken to the front of the church to be presented to the missionary. Because we were at the back of the church, my father's business card was on top. The missionary picked it out of the collection plate and visibly blanched. He looked up and searched the crowd until he found us sitting near the back.

After a weak smile, he took the podium. His talk was short, and he said very little about the "important work." The church's minister was obviously confused, because he expected the missionary to take more time and get the congregation excited about the "important work." My family left at the end of the service without saying a word to anyone.

Missionaries have made a lot of money by selling themselves as the saviors of starving Africans, especially Ethiopians. At no point do they mention that Ethiopia (in particular) is a lush and bountiful country quite capable of self-sustenance, or that the starvation of the 1970s and 1980s was caused by decimation of crops directly related to the introduction of large, non-indigenous herds of cattle that were being fed the grains that normally sustained humans, or that the cattle was being exported to Angola, Russia, and other communist-dominated countries rather than feeding the local population.

So… back to the Macy's story.

I decided to go to the slide show. It began with some pictures of vegetation. The woman, let's call her Wendy, said that it was the most horrible place she'd ever been. It was hotter than anything she'd ever experienced and everyone was hot and sweaty all the time. Her slides reminded me of South Carolina with its thick, verdant hillsides and oversized floral blossoms, and I said so. In fact her description of high heat and high humidity reminded me of South Carolina or Florida in the summer. My comparison clearly made her uncomfortable and a bit flustered. Not having been to either of those places, she didn't know how to react. She stared at me in silence, causing the first uncomfortable moment during her presentation.

She then showed pictures of the compound where her family stayed and the current missionaries lived. She showed the gate and said that the compound had to be gated because the locals were all thieves and stole anything and everything. She told how the missionaries had once received a refrigerator and left it out on the porch. Next thing they knew, it was gone.

Then she talked about how weird it was because at the same time locals would give you anything they had. She told about a beautiful scarf she saw a woman wearing. When she complimented the woman on the scarf, the woman took it off and gave it to her. She refused it, but the woman wouldn't relent and insisted that she should have it. She finally accepted it, just to make the woman stop.

Then Wendy went on to say that Mozambique had been much better off under Portuguese rule and that, since liberation in 1975, it had become a chaotic and miserable place with no law or order, as evidenced by the thievery. I tried to counter her assertions with facts about the brutality of Portuguese rule. Again, my comments clearly made people uncomfortable. This woman was their friend and I was calling her out. And I was aware that I was the only person of color in the room, and apparently the only one with the slightest amount of knowledge about history. Still, I was uncomfortable with it. I later mentioned to a manager that I thought it was an incredibly racist presentation and was shocked that she was permitted to give it without any vetting. The response was silence.

Now for some deconstruction. Let's start with the story from the 1960s. Whether it's about Africans or about African-Americans there are always white people ready to profiteer by projecting an image of us as helpless and unable to care for ourselves. Even the so-called welfare system in the U.S. was built on a model of white salvation. Hundreds of millions, maybe billions, of dollars went into that system, but from 1965 and well into the 1990s the majority of that money went to pay salaries for social workers and the bureaucrats who ran the system, almost all of whom were white. When people of color finally rose to positions of influence in the 1980s and 1990s, "welfare" became a dirty word and suddenly systems were being shut down. Imagine what could have happened had that money been put directly into the hands of the African Americans who, for generations and without support, still managed to provide basic education for children, own and operate businesses, and survive while in the crosshairs of racism. But that would have gone against the vision white people have of themselves as saviors. It would have gone against the white supremacist view that people of color, especially African Americans, are childlike and unable to care for ourselves.

The fact is that we don't need a savior. What we need is for white people to get out of our way. Each time they have, we have proven ourselves more than capable. Think: Dr. Daniel Hale Williams, Neil DeGrasse Tyson, Mae Jemison, Serena and Venus Williams, Tiger Woods, the Tuskegee Airmen, Thurgood Marshall, Oprah Winfrey, Jackie Robinson. Just give us the resources we need and get out of our way. And if we screw it up, how are we any different than white people? They've had the power all these generations and what have they done with it? What can we possibly do worse?

The Macy's story is a bit more disturbing to me than the one of the 1960s. "Wendy" was received among her white peers as an "expert." She had *been* to Africa. She was *born* there and had ties there. *Of course*, she knew what she was talking about, right? Well, no, actually, she didn't. Here's why.

First, she clearly didn't understand customs in the country of her birth (a clue to what kind of missionaries her parents were). There are many cultures that don't value ownership, including indigenous people on our very own continent. If the refrigerator she mentioned was sitting on a porch, it may have been seen as an indication that it was not being used, and therefore available to someone who had need of it. You know... like we put things out on the curbside in front of our houses for people to take for free. Only Wendy couldn't make the connection because she saw the nature, culture, and people in Mozambique through a racist filter that indicated they had negative intent. She was unable to make the connection between the scarf she was given, simply because she admired it and the owner had no more need of it, and the refrigerator.

Second, Wendy's belief that Portuguese rule was better than independence was an obvious outgrowth of her role as a privileged white person. During that era, white people could steal, rape, murder and commit other crimes, especially against the indigenous population, without suffering the same fate as locals. Portugal was one of the most brutal and brutish colonial masters on every continent. The punishments they applied against indigenous people were macabre and violent. Theft resulted in chopping off of limbs. Forced labor was the norm. All of the laws of pre-independence Mozambique were made to protect white people and their interests. Where colonial laws conflicted with local custom and indigenous law, white people's needs always prevailed.

Any of this feel familiar? It should. It's what journalist Charles Mudede keeps trying to explain and what generations of activists on this continent have been saying before him: the laws are written to comply with a white world view of property and power. Every official role that's been created is intended to enforce and protect that worldview.

Here's a recent example. In August 2014 a police officer tasered a Christopher Lollie, who was just sitting on a bench waiting for his children to come out of day care, because a shop owner called saying there was "someone suspicious" sitting in front of his shop. The officer responded aggressively to the need to protect a white person's property. Had the need been to actually enforce law and keep peace, the dispatcher would have simply asked the caller what the person was doing that raised suspicion. If the caller responded, "He's sitting on a bench," the dispatcher would have known not to send an officer. If the dispatch had happened anyway, the officer would have politely explained that there had been report of someone suspicious in the area and then asked Mr. Lollie, and everyone else in the area, why they were there. Instead, the very presence of a young black man was seen as a threat to white property by the shop owner, the dispatcher, and the police officer. All assumed negative intent. None respected his humanity enough to simply ask.

Returning to Wendy… most disturbing of all was her role as an interpreter of a culture she's barely familiar with. People at Macy's looked up to her. They were her longtime friends and shared her narrow world experience. Her language and tone reinforced their beliefs that anything African-related was to be treated as inferior. They presumed that because she had been to Africa, she must know. Only my presence, as a counter-narrator, jarred that experience. How often, though, is there no person of color in the room to enter the challenge? And for the person of color who happens upon this experience, it is an exhausting role to play. We're often told to "pick your battles," but each battle has consequences. I had to continue to work with these people, and Wendy's reinforcement of their beliefs of white cultural superiority would have a daily impact on my ability to effectively do my job. Silence was not an option I could afford.

We actually don't need white people to speak on our behalf. We are capable of doing it ourselves. Again, they just need to get out of the way. If you want to know what we think, ask us. Since, like white people, we come in variety packs, be sure to get more than one opinion. But get it from us, not from someone who "grew up with black people," or "has lots of black friends," or worse yet "has a black friend who says…" Don't even presume that someone married to a person of color has the right to speak for that person's experience.

Also, recognize how really stupid white people often seem to us. Wendy clearly didn't know Mozambique's cultural practices or history. She may seem heroic to her small circle of similarly insulated friends and co-workers, but someday she's going to encounter someone who actually knows something about the political and cultural history she's misrepresenting, and she's going to look like an idiot. This was the case with the "spoken word" woman I described in the first essay about culture. White people in the U.S. know very little history or culture outside their own little tiny circles. My mother, who received a high school education in Sudan, spoke seven languages, understood the developmental history of every continent, and could speak at length and depth on historical figures from every continent. Her U.S. contemporaries spoke one language (sometimes roughly), knew only the version of history that made the U.S. heroic, and knew little, if anything, about the geniuses of the rest of the world.

My hope, again, sits with white Millennials, but they have to choose: will they explore and learn the broad lessons of world history in order to find a new path for humanity, or will they continue to insularly shape a path just for themselves, focused on their own material satisfaction? Will they claim and use their privilege to save themselves, or recognize that they could partner with the rest of humanity to save us all? Only time will tell.

5. LIBERALS (AND THEIR PROGRESSIVE COUSINS)

When I was six, my father had a series of heart attacks. The high mountain altitude of Addis Ababa was too hard on his already-enlarged, Galveston-sea-level-raised physiology. Our family packed up and moved 12,000 miles to Berkeley, CA to be close to my father's sister. Though their family roots were in Texas, she had moved to Berkeley and established a business as a grocer in nearby Oakland. After eight months living with her, we moved to a small suburb twenty miles south, where we were one of six black families in a population of 10,000. Four of the families lived across town and only one of their kids, five years older than me, attended public school. The other family lived two blocks away and their children were a decade younger than my brother or me.

Winter of 1958 I started third grade in this community. There was no National Guard. There was no support from the Federal government. I just walked around the corner from my house and into hell every day. I could write volumes about the harassment and daily indignities: the bullying and degradation by students, teachers and parents. That's not what I'm writing about here though—anyway not right now—so I'll just say that survival was all I could hope for and what I clung to. I went from being a high-status child in a healthy, loving environment attending a parochial school in Ethiopia (run by nuns who were kind, gentle, and loving), to being a bottom-status pariah that no one wanted to associate with in a Northern California school during an era that touted the West Coast as the bastion of liberalism and tolerance.

A few days into the first month of school, one of the girls in class walked around putting pieces of paper on people's desks. Thinking it was some kind of class assignment, I waited to get mine. The teacher noticed that the student was passing out the paper and, in full voice, in front of the class, asked what she was doing. The girl, whose family lived directly across the street from mine, explained that she was passing out invitations to her birthday party. Everyone was invited, she said, except for me. That was the tone of the next decade of my life.

There were white kids in my neighborhood who were not openly hostile, but few were friendly. And those who were friendly attended private school and treated me with pitiable tolerance. In this atmosphere, I became friends with a Chinese-American girl and a Japanese-American girl. Carolyn, Patty and I were the outsiders: the brown girls. The exotic.

We walked to school together every single day from third grade through high school. We did everything together: movies, Girl Scouts, homework. From third through eighth grade they were my only friends, and I theirs.

High school classes split us apart, so we didn't spend as much time together. I became friends with a white girl for the first time. She was smart, irreverent, unbound by convention. Like me, she liked math and science as well as writing and drama. She came from a politically and religiously liberal family. They were tolerant. She and I talked about everything: school, boys, music, boys, politics, boys, religion, bo... well, you get the idea. Truth be told, though, I kept my feelings and thoughts about boys mostly to myself. I learned early on that boys who were in any way associated with me were quickly shunned, so I learned to show no feelings about them. Mona was one of the few people I trusted with my crushes. She pulled me into the outer circle of her friends, who tolerated me on her behalf.

I had skipped a grade in Ethiopia (long story for another time), so the kids in my grade were older than me. Although Mona's birthday was just days away from mine, she was a year older. As her 16th birthday approached we spent hours planning her party. For over a month we labored over the details: invitation list, cake, music for dancing, games we would play. When Mona telephoned a couple of days before the party, I thought it was to discuss yet another detail or the RSVPs. Instead, she called to let me know that I couldn't come to her party. Several of the other guests' parents, led by one of the members of her liberal church, had contacted her parents to let them know that if I attended the party, their children would not. With apologies, I was uninvited from the party.

And there, ladies and gentlemen, was my first introduction to the internal politics of white liberals. It was fine for me to plan the party, down to the last details, but if the choice was between me coming to the party or appeasing other white people, the choice was simple. I believe Ron Sims knows something about this on a grand scale, eh Ron? Good enough to run the largest county in the state, but gotta wait your turn, after the white girl, to run for governor.

It was a long time before I internalized this lesson. A very long time. And my psyche has scorch marks to prove it. This, for me, is the line of demarcation between liberals and true progressives (though I have some warnings to come there as well). Liberals will encourage me to set the fire, they will fan the flames, they will suggest I step into it while they hold the hose, but the second the cops show up they'll drop that hose and insist they were just passers-by. In the Jesus story, for example, Peter was a liberal. I could write an entire treatise on why the church founded under his guidance is as screwed up as he was, but that, again, would take a forever or two and I don't actually care right now.

I have many, many, many white liberal friends. Few have ever stepped into the fire. I expect few ever will. They'll get just close enough to say they were there when the stories are told later down the line. They might even have a few singe marks where a stray ember caught their clothing. I know that many of these friends will abandon me in crisis. Some will even turn on me to save themselves. I've in fact seen this play out already in my life. They will protect their jobs, their familial ties, their sense of security, their prosperity, and their social standing before they'll fight for me. When the battle is over they'll return with "I knew you could do it!" or "Wow, that was really something" or some other foolishness.

A few *will* surprise me and show extraordinary courage of conviction, teaching me, and themselves, about the depth of their character. However, while the brothers, cousins, nephews, sons, fathers, uncles and other men of my community die, most white liberals will wring their hands, tsk-tsk a few times, and wonder why nobody does anything to stop the murder of innocent boys and men. You, dear liberal friends, are the ones who *can* do something. But will you step into the fire? How much are you willing to scorch? Only person I'm willing to take bets on this with is Ron Sims.

{*An epilogue: The parents who were responsible for me not going to Mona's birthday party showed up in my office 40 years later where I was an executive in the headquarters of their liberal religion. Squirming commenced. I talked about the racist town I grew up in. She and her hubby pretended we'd never met. Oh, and that liberal religion... yup, played out true to form. Threw me into the fire and let me burn. 'Course, by then, I was asbestos-clad.*}

My lessons on progressives came in multiple experiences while I worked for said liberal religious organization. I guess it's important to say this: my job was to work with activists across the country, from mainly progressive affiliates, to create a program that would train and support them in their work.

Here's one example of what I learned:

The man who hired me was the former minister of a congregation I once belonged to. He needed someone with my background in developing training programs, and knew from experience that I was an active opponent of oppression. After I was hired, but before I started the new job, he showed me where my office would be. It was a tiny space, no more than 8'x10', but the window overlooked the Boston Common.

The room looked even smaller, because it had been used as storage space, with an old credenza stuffed with papers and topped with boxes along one wall, and floor-to-ceiling shelving filled with books and boxes along the opposite wall. A large, dark, wooden, formal desk bisected the tiny space. Boxes were stacked between the desk and the entrance to the room. He assured me the office would be emptied by the time I started work, six weeks later. He also asked if the furniture suited me. I asked that it be replaced by a small round table, a small lateral file cabinet, and a cabinet-style desk. He assured me that his assistant, a middle-aged white woman who I'd met briefly earlier that day, would take care of all the details.

Six weeks later I arrived for work and went straight to my office, which was exactly as it had been six weeks earlier. Not one box had been moved, not one bit of space cleared. I couldn't even get to the other side of the desk. My new boss arrived to find me staring into the room in bewilderment. If I'd had any sense, I would have walked out and never returned. Instead, I asked when the office would be ready for me to occupy and when my new furniture would be arriving. He asked his assistant. She said she had been too busy to deal with it. He made no attempt to hold her accountable or demand that she do her job. It was left to me to shuffle things around so that I could get to the desk.

A few days later, in a gesture of goodwill, I invited the assistant to lunch. We went to a place she identified as her favorite Mexican restaurant. Five minutes after we were seated, she said these words to me (seared in my memory): "I will never do what you want. I don't work for you, and I don't care about you. I work for the same boss you do. You need something done, you'll have to do it yourself." It was a tense lunch.

My boss was out of town on that day, but when he returned I told him about the lunch and asked for his advice. When he asked her about our lunch, she denied having said anything negative to me and insisted that I "must have misunderstood." He then told me I must have misunderstood her because she was really a nice person and he couldn't imagine her saying anything like that. I ended up emptying the office, buying the furniture, and installing it myself. Yes, I should have run… fast.

For six years I complained numerous times about this woman's harassment and insubordination, and submitted my specific and detailed complaints to my boss and to human resources. My white, male boss repeatedly protected his white, female assistant and left me to fend for myself. The assistant complained that she was intimidated by me, yet I had never yelled at her, never been violent toward her, never done anything other than asked her to do her job.

Eventually she, like the man I worked with at Macy's, extended her harassment to a few white women. When *they* complained, action was taken, and it was instant. She was fired. Had she been a woman of color, treating an executive with that level of disrespect, she wouldn't have lasted a week. I stayed in that job because I loved the work I was doing. I spent as much time as possible on the road, working with local activists. I dreaded each time I returned to the central office.

From this experience I learned that white progressives take care of their own, and only their own. They are as cruel and dogmatic as ultraconservatives, only they smile in your face while twisting the knife in your back. Unlike ultraconservatives, progressives have deluded themselves into believing they love everybody, but that love is theoretical and crumbles easily when put to the test.

That was why, while many of my black friends were blindsided by progressives' reaction to the #BlackLivesMatter interruption of Bernie Sanders' speech at Westlake Center in Seattle, I was not. White cultural supremacy sits just under the surface of progressives' beliefs about how the world should be, and they will enforce their dogma with equal violence.

6. Slavery Was A Long Time Ago

Conversations where white people do discuss race, especially when they don't believe there are people of color present, go something like this:

"I'm not a racist. Hell, I had nothing to do with slavery. My family had nothing to do with slavery. Bad things happened to black people a long time ago... so what's that got to do with me? Black people need to just get over it."

Most white people seem to believe that racism is something they have to actively sign up to do. They confuse prejudice (liking one thing over another) with racism (a system of policies and instilled habits that gives white people political, cultural, economic and other advantages).

A racist isn't someone who hates people based on the color of their skin. A racist is the beneficiary of the theory of race, someone who benefits economically, socially, politically, and culturally from the theory of Caucasian racial superiority.

I offer here an exercise for those white people who believe racism has nothing to do with their current place in the world, especially those who believe they are successful based on their merits alone.

Step 1: Create a social history map of your family. Instead of the traditional family tree that tracks lineage via births and deaths, this map will identify significant events that impacted or reflected your family's change in social status. These events may include significant births, deaths, residential moves, employment opportunities (promotions/demotions), purchase of a house, educational advancement, economic losses, etc. The resulting change in status might be in a positive or negative direction (e.g.: prolonged unemployment, stock market crash).

To give you some ideas, I've created an abbreviated social history of my family up to my graduation from high school. There are many significant events that didn't make my map because they didn't change the family's social status. For example, I briefly attended a parochial school in Berkeley, CA. While that had significant impact on me individually, it didn't change my family's social status in any way, so it's not on the map.

As you will see, this is quite different from a family tree. It does take a lot of time to do, maybe several sittings, so relax into it. If you know there was a general status shift, but don't know specifically what caused it, give it a generally identifying name. For example, if you know that your great-grandmother "came into money" but don't know whether the source was from an inheritance, sale of property, or backyard moonshine still, just use something generic like "Granny came into money."

Once you're satisfied all of the major status shifts in your family have been identified, continue to the next step.

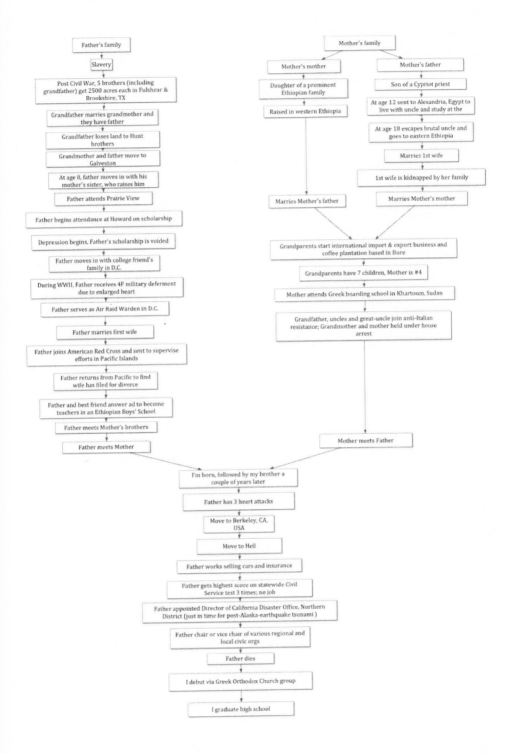

Father's family
- Slavery
- Post Civil War, 5 brothers (including grandfather) get 2500 acres each in Fulshear & Brookshire, TX
- Grandfather marries grandmother and they have father
- Grandfather loses land to Hunt brothers
- Grandmother and father move to Galveston
- At age 8, father moves in with his mother's sister, who raises him
- Father attends Prairie View
- Father begins attendance at Howard on scholarship
- Depression begins, Father's scholarship is voided
- Father moves in with college friend's family in D.C.
- During WWII, Father receives 4F military deferment due to enlarged heart
- Father serves as Air Raid Warden in D.C.
- Father marries first wife
- Father joins American Red Cross and sent to supervise efforts in Pacific Islands
- Father returns from Pacific to find wife has filed for divorce
- Father and best friend answer ad to become teachers in an Ethiopian Boys' School
- Father meets Mother's brothers
- Father meets Mother

Mother's family

Mother's mother
- Daughter of a prominent Ethiopian family
- Raised in western Ethiopia
- Marries Mother's father

Mother's father
- Son of a Cypriot priest
- At age 12 sent to Alexandria, Egypt to live with uncle and study at the
- At age 18 escapes brutal uncle and goes to eastern Ethiopia
- Marries 1st wife
- 1st wife is kidnapped by her family
- Marries Mother's mother

- Grandparents start international import & export business and coffee plantation based in Bure
- Grandparents have 7 children, Mother is #4
- Mother attends Greek boarding school in Khartoum, Sudan
- Grandfather, uncles and great-uncle join anti-Italian resistance; Grandmother and mother held under house arrest

Mother meets Father

- I'm born, followed by my brother a couple of years later
- Father has 3 heart attacks
- Move to Berkeley, CA, USA
- Move to Hell
- Father works selling cars and insurance
- Father gets highest score on statewide Civil Service test 3 times; no job
- Father appointed Director of California Disaster Office, Northern District (just in time for post-Alaska-earthquake tsunami)
- Father chair or vice chair of various regional and local civic orgs
- Father dies
- I debut via Greek Orthodox Church group
- I graduate high school

-31-

Step 2: Identify those events in your family social history map that required resources and identify those resources. Resources can be education, money or other economic assets, people, knowledge, political connections, etc.

I've done this with a segment of my family's social history as a sample. The status changes that were dependent on resources are in the shaded boxes on the left. The resources they required are on the right.

After you've identified the resources, continue to Step 3.

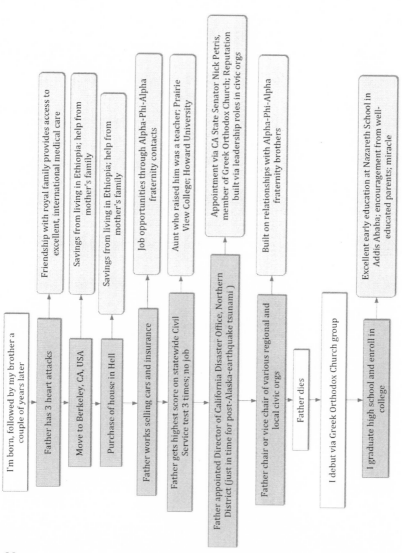

Step 3: Review the resources you identified. Were they available to everybody, or were there people who were excluded by law, practice or custom? For example, if your great-grandmother started her own business, using funds borrowed from a bank or from other family members, was this possible for everyone? If not, who was excluded? If you don't know, take time to research and find out.

I've done this with an abbreviated segment of my family's social history as a sample.

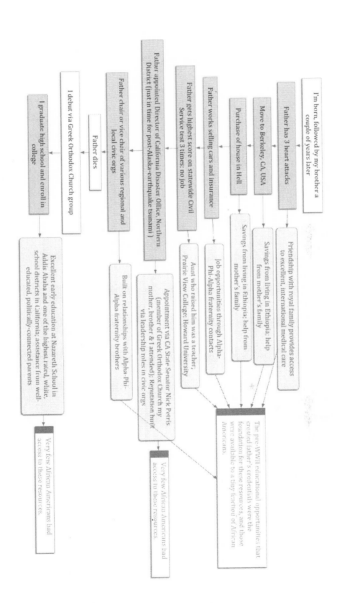

So far you've (a) identified the key points of your family's change in social status (b) recognized the resources it took to make those changes, and (c) determined who did or did not have access to those resources. Now, at each step, imagine what would have happened to your family if they had not had access to those resources. Follow the cascade of events. For example, in my family's scenario, if my parents didn't have a relationship to the Ethiopian royal family, my father probably would have died in Ethiopia. We would have never moved to the United States. Like the rest of my mother's family, we would have been displaced when the royal family was overthrown and probably have ended up in Greece.

If you are white, imagine what the impact would have been on your family if they had been of African, or Asian, Native American, or Latino descent. What if they hadn't been able to get the bank loan to buy their first home? What if the community they actually moved into had restrictive covenants that didn't allow anyone who wasn't white... how would that have impacted the education of future generations? What if the jobs they had were not available to people of color, how would that impact the location of their home, their ability to pursue higher education, access to health care, and overall economic progress?

If you are a person of color, imagine the impact on your family if they had access to resources readily available to whites.

The gap between what was available to white families and was available to those who were in oppressed racial groups is the measure of racism and its outcome: privilege.

It's obvious that my African American experience is vastly atypical. I confess to great class privilege before arriving in the U.S., and that has translated into much lifelong privilege and much responsibility. I have achieved many things in my life, but none of those would have been possible without the very privileged ladder that was built before my birth. However, much of that early class-based privilege evaporated the moment I set foot on U.S. soil. My African and African-American ancestry trumped my education and economic access. Over time, my light skin color opened doors to opportunities not afforded to people with more brown in the their skin pigment. That door shut as soon as I revealed my ancestry, which I have learned to do early in every personal and professional setting.

The mythology of the self-made person is a lie. We make one another. There are people much smarter than I am and much more gifted who are invisible simply because we live in a society that doesn't allow them to fully develop their gifts, that actively withholds resources from them.

Recently I heard Rev. Jesse Jackson say this:

> *We never knew how good baseball could be until everyone could play. We never knew how good basketball could be until everyone could play. We never knew how good football could be until everyone could play at every level.*

Millions of babies' lives have been saved because of the breakthrough surgical techniques developed by African American Dr. Vivien Thomas. How many others could be contributing if only they had the opportunity? Is the cure to breast cancer secreted in the mind of a young African American boy or girl whose curiosity gets them sent to detention instead of college? Is the next breakthrough in environmental sustainability beating in the heart of a young Native American boy or girl who understands the movement of the stars in a way not considered before, but who has no one to mentor and guide them? How much do we lose as a society, and as a species, by putting all of our resources in the hands of one group of people?

If your racial identity has created opportunities for you that weren't available to others, then you are a racist, a beneficiary of racism. *You* are the problem.

7. WHITE EXCEPTIONS TO RACISM

In the first essay of this book, I referred to the incident in Seattle when a young African American man was pepper-sprayed by a mall security guard. The young man was on his way to meet a friend for lunch when he had to pass through a crowd of white men and women protesting the U.S. position against Palestine. They were gathered in a plaza adjacent to the mall. A white man was violently accosting and attacking the protesters. At one point he held another white man by the throat. When the security guard came out of the mall into the plaza, the violent white man had his shirt off and was screaming at the young African American man, who was simply trying to walk through the plaza. Without hesitation, the security guard pepper-sprayed the young African American man, pinned him against a wall, and attempted to arrest him. The white protesters kept screaming to the security guard that he had the wrong man, that it was the white man who was dangerous. He ignored them. When a white police officer arrived, he immediately sided with the security guard, further victimizing the young man. A white man who happened to be filming for the protesters caught it all on video.

A conversation about the incident was quickly organized by staff from the Northwest Film Forum to take place at their movie house days later. A panel of speakers was recruited. Since the planners were white, I walked in expecting a panel consisting of white protesters, the white videographer, a representative from the security company, and maybe a representative from the police department. I wanted to hear what they experienced and how they felt about being eyewitnesses to racism as it violated an innocent black man and validated a violent white man. Since the protesters prided themselves as activists fighting oppression, I wanted to know what they were going to do about this situation right in their own backyard.

Instead, the panel consisted of nine African Americans. The audience was mainly white. Each panelist spoke about the deep trauma being experienced by African Americans in the ongoing video-confirmation of racism from across the country. The final panelist, Christa Bell, turned the tables and said she wanted to hear from the audience. By then, I was mad. I was fuming. I was tired of African Americans putting our trauma on display for white people to cluck their tongues and say "how awful" it all was. I said so. I expressed my frustration that white people were not taking any responsibility for this conversation.

A white woman was seated next to me. She raised her hand and used the opportunity to let everyone know that she wasn't "that kind of white person" and that the actions of the security guard didn't reflect her beliefs. She just wanted us to all love one another and stop focusing on our differences.

Over the past year we've repeatedly reached that place where people of color are spilling our guts, wrestling with our dignity in a series of public efforts to give white people the reasons to stand up to one another and demand a reframing of the racial insanity that permeates our culture. At workshops, meetings, and "conversations," on TV, radio, and social media people of color, especially African Americans, are being asked "How do you feel?" or "What do you think?" about yet another innocent murdered by law enforcement or at the hands of a white supremacist. And, repeatedly, we've reached that place where white people demand that they be seen as the innocents in this narrative, insisting, "I'm not like those white people." By turning the focus back on themselves they attempt to prove that people of color are imperfect for blaming them, therefore they can negate everything we say or demand.

So... to all the white people who believe you are an exception to the oppression of people of color:

You know that frustration you feel because you're not "that kind of white person?" Sit with that frustration for a while. Really feel it, deeply. Does it make you angry to get dismissed and clumped into a whole group of people you have no control over? Yup... sit with that anger. How often do you feel that frustration? Daily, weekly, monthly, yearly? Only when you're around people of color talking about race (and how often is that)? How often do you feel that anger of being mis-associated? Oh, and the helplessness from not being able to do anything about it... how often do you feel that?

Understand: THAT is the feeling black people and other people of color live with every minute of every day. AND for us it's not just a feeling: it's a matter of life or death. What a random person of color thinks of a white person seldom has any repercussions: personal, professional or otherwise. You are more at risk with other white people than with us. You are more likely to be robbed, raped, murdered, assaulted, or scammed by a white person than by any people of color. However, what a random white person thinks of a person of color is always a matter of life and death. The moment you feel uncomfortable with one of us, our life is in danger. If not our lives, then certainly our livelihoods.

It's why in this age we still experience store security following us. Why Forest Whitaker can be publicly frisked in a New York deli while one of Seattle's major white, female, TV anchors can shoplift at will for decades and never spend a minute being harassed. In fact everyone conspires to keep her secret instead of naming her a thief. It's why a white shop clerk can call police to harass a black man who is simply sitting on a bench, waiting to pick up his children from school, and get an instant response.

So stop whining about being exceptional, exempt. You're not. Ever.

8. Ass-u-me

Spring of 1998, I packed up all my belongings, put them in storage, and left Boston to return home, to Seattle. My brother, sister-in-law, mother were all living on Vashon Island, so I drove cross-country (via the Grand Canyon) and settled on the island.

A few months after my arrival, several race-related incidents on island drove me to write an op-ed for the local newspaper, the Beachcomber. The major incident was simple: a sex offender had been released and was living on island. This particular sex offender happened to be black. A story about him was in the Beachcomber. A few days later, another black man was standing in line at the Island Thriftway when a woman started yelling at him, saying she knew who he was and people like him weren't wanted on the island. This man, an island resident having no relationship to the sex offender, had no idea what she was talking about.

The story of this incident opened the door for stories of other incidents. For example, an elementary school teacher gave a black student an F on a report because the "historically significant leader" the student chose to write his essay about was Malcolm X, who the teacher decided did not fit her criteria.

Following my op-ed, I received a phone call from a white man I'd never met but who lived on the island. He wondered whether I could make some time to meet with him and talk a bit more about my op-ed. After talking with my brother and a few other island residents, I decided this guy was safe and I agreed to meet him for coffee.

We greeted one another with a handshake and went through the normal introductions and chit-chat. He then told me that he had a proposition for me. These are not great words for a white man to start a conversation with a black woman of my era (unless, of course, you're flirting and there have been clear signals of welcome… you know who you are). This is not a man I flirted with or had any interest in flirting with. Apprehensively, I asked about the nature of the proposition.

He explained that he had just started a new business, and he thought I might be interested. The business? {Wait for it…} The business was legal insurance. I'd never heard of legal insurance, so I asked what it was. Apparently there is insurance you can buy in case you might get arrested sometime in the future and need legal assistance. The legal insurance will supposedly cover some of your legal fees and guarantee representation.

I stopped breathing, because if I had breathed the language that would have come out of my mouth… well, you know… angry black woman stuff. In slow, measured language I asked him why he thought I was a good candidate for legal insurance. I asked what in the op-ed indicated I might have a need for legal insurance.

Oh he hemmed and hawed. He suggested that even if I didn't foresee any need for his services, perhaps some of my family or friends would, and maybe I could tell them about his business. I explained that none of my family on either side had ever been arrested (well, except by the Italians during the Ethiopian resistance, but he didn't need to know that), and that few of my friends were likely to be arrested. I was speaking through gritted teeth. Wouldn't be surprised if he heard hissing.

At some point it occurred to him that he'd made a mistake. A deep mistake that was more than just an oops. I quickly ended the meeting and left, seething. Yet again, a white person had made assumptions about not just who I am, but my character and the character of all those I associate with. I wondered how many of his white friends on the island he had approached with this same proposition. I happen to know that some of them had family with arrest records.

Next, here's another quick Macy's story. A white man on the Diversity Committee was married to a black woman who also worked for the company. At one meeting he missed, one of the white women on the committee started talking about the number of people of color on the committee. As she named them, she listed this white man. I stopped her and said, "He's not black." She said "Well, he's half black." I said, "No, I know his background and his family ancestry is all Scottish and Irish." "Well," she said, "He's half black." Apparently she had decided to extend the one-drop rule to him. I had noticed that, although this man had seniority and regularly out-performed his peers statistically, he was often passed over for awards and promotions. Guilt by association.

Now, a more recent story. This past spring I attended a meeting with a dozen or so people from the local arts sector. We were discussing a large-scale project one of them had conceived and wanted help bringing to fruition. I was the only black participant. A few weeks after the meeting I received an email from one of the other participants, the founder of a large, local arts organization. The purpose of her email: to ask me to meet with her to discuss my potential support of her latest project. She planned to start a charter school in one of the poorest, largely African American, parts of the city. The 6-12th grade school would focus on STEAM subjects (Science, Technology, Engineering, Arts, and Math). She didn't live in the community. She didn't have, and had not sought, any grassroots support from the local community for the project. She had just decided to do this and presumed it would be a welcome project.

My response to her request: Not only would I *not* support her project, I would actively work against it. Why? Because there are organizations that have been serving that community with no resources and no assistance for decades. Efforts that were locally seeded and supported were scraping by. This woman, with her clout and white privilege would drain every tiny bit of resource away from these hard-working, committed projects led by people within the community. If she truly wanted to serve the community, she would have done some research to find existing projects in line with her desire to help and then brought them her clout and resources so they could expand and grow.

Where black people experience trauma, vultures see economic opportunity. We have seen this in the "poor, starving children" commercials that always lead to white-led organizations that spend the majority of their funds paying themselves. History showed this to us in the development of Welfare programs of the 1960s through the 1980s, where the majority of recipients from program dollars were program managers and staff, and not those in need.

This form of micro-aggression shows up as white people posing as saviors, as speakers-on-behalf-of, as explainers. Other white people give them praise, glory, and lots of money for it, thus perpetuating the myth, while people of color, who actually have standing and credibility, get cut out of access to resources. It's time to hold people accountable.

White people's unfounded assumptions about people of color create absurd behaviors. They end up getting burned in their own fires, and then blame us for the heat. Insane.

9. Why Do They Hate Us?

After the February 2001 Nisqually earthquake, I got a cell phone. As much as I love technology, I'm not an early adopter, waiting, instead, for the gadget to prove itself necessary. But after the earthquake, I saw the need to be able to reach my elderly mother and out-of-state brother.

So, on that crystal-clear, sun kissed, bird-call-filled morning, in September I stuck my cell phone in my purse and headed north on the Vashon Highway toward the ferry dock and work. I turned the radio to NPR, expecting the wake-up voices of their morning show and finding panic-ridden, grief-stricken versions instead.

What? What did he just say? What? What?

Once my brain processed the words I pulled to the side of the road sobbing. Oh no. No. Were we at war? I dialed the cell and reached my just-waking mother.

"It's finally happened." I sobbed into the receiver.

"What? What's happened? What's wrong?"

"Do you have your TV on? Turn your TV on." I must have been nearly screaming.

She saw the images before I did.

"Oh, no!" was her response.

"It finally happened," I cried. "All these years we knew it would. And now it has. Someone has finally had enough."

I knew I had to keep going to work. Knew this incident would be the core of my day, no matter what else had been planned. The surreal day turned into a surreal week; week to month; month to year; year to decade.

As I reached out to friends, a pattern emerged in their responses. Most white people asked, over and over, "Why would anyone hate us so much." People of color and progressive white people said, "Chickens come home to roost." Though I had spent nearly a decade in the world of social justice activists and should have known better, I still harbored the hope that this horrific event would create the opportunity for honest dialog about our nation's policies around the world and the racist tactics our government has used to achieve them. Instead we got caught up on what to call fried potatoes and whether to buy imported cheese.

That diversion was no accident. In order to talk intelligently about "Why do they hate us," the general white public would have had to know something about the world and their place in it. But their brains had been filled with chasing the Lexus dream, or celebrating Elvis' birthday, or little blue pills, or the sex lives of athletes. Their priorities focused on appearances rather than reality.

To most white people, the good ole U.S. of A. appeared to be the world's benevolent grandpa. Therefore it must be so. We gave all those cute little third-world, oops, uh, "developing" countries money every time they shed a teardrop in our direction, right? We stood for democracy around the world, right? We helped little countries become more economically viable with our trade opportunities, right? We saved Europe from Hitler, dammit, and they're *still* grateful, even the French, right?

But history has shown that even benevolent appearing grandpas can be malicious, sadistic, child molesters. Our country has left a gouge on every continent.

- We are responsible for drawing many of the post-WWII national borders in Africa, the Middle East, and Europe without input from the actual people who lived there.
- Israel did not exist as a physical nation until our country, Britain, and France drew lines on a map and declared that everyone who lived inside those lines belonged to this new nation, existing residents be damned. Not very democratic of us.
- Using covert operations in Central and South America we installed vicious, sadistic leaders and then fed them barrels full of our taxpayer money that they used for personal gain while imprisoning, killing, and otherwise terrorizing the populace.
- While touting the virtues of democracy, our government liberated the Philippines Islands from Spain and turned them into yet another dictatorship.

- Batista, Marcos, Pinochet, Hussein, Somoza, Noriega, Pahlavi… all dictators put in place by U.S. military and covert operations.
- Throughout Asia and the Pacific Islands we set up military bases, in the name of national security, where our military personnel raped and abused the local populations of places like Subic Bay and Yokohama.

Have you ever had your car stolen? Your home burgled? Been assaulted? How long does it take to recover from that sense of violation? How long to feel trust toward strangers? If the violator has been identified, how do you feel about them? What do you want done to them?

So imagine this: imagine that you're a young boy hearing stories from your grandmother about how your family once lived in a lovely little home surrounded other family members. Then one day these people came along with guns and told them they all had to leave or die. Your family was moved to a tent in a country where the customs were different and they no longer had a home or the ability to find work or find a place to call their own. In search of security the family members were driven apart. The weapons held by the people who displaced your family all came from this place called the United States of America.

Or this: you're a 13-year-old boy with blonde hair, blue eyes, brown skin, who is a foot taller than anyone in your village. When people look at you, you see pity (or is that hate) in their eyes. Even your mother holds you at a distance. After years of confusion, your mother finally tells you that she was sold to Americans as a sex slave when she was the age you are now, and became pregnant with you at 15.

Or this: you're a 10-year-old boy and your father has disappeared. Your uncle disappeared the month before. Your other uncle has been missing for several months. Your mother hides your older brother under a pile of clothes whenever anyone comes to the door. One day soldiers march into your village. They gather your grandfather, your brother, and all the men and older boys at the village's edge, accuse them of trying to overthrow the government, and shoot them all. The government has tens of thousands of weapons, and millions of dollars they pay to informants, who make up information just to get paid. All of the weapons are from the United States of America. The money to pay the informants comes from the United States of America.

In 1995, I joined a fact-finding group with the Racial Justice Working Group of the U.S. National Council of Churches on a trip to Juarez, just over the Mexican border from El Paso, Texas. We saw dozens of huge manufacturing plants, many of them making microprocessors for major U.S. companies. We met with Mexicans whose family roots in Juarez went back many generations. They took us into their small, dirt-floor, tidy homes and prepared a huge, delicious feast for the dozen or so people in our group. They took us to an area just a few blocks from their block of homes where we saw a huge, adobe-walled area that was a full block around. Standing in front of the walled area, at a solid iron gate were two black-clothed guards holding automatic weapons. Above them, atop the gate and at each corner of the block, were cameras.

What was this? Was this a compound of some sort? No. It was a residence. One residence. Who lived there? A manager, brought from the U.S. to oversee plant operations. What an eyesore! Yes, but there was more. That residence was built where there had once been a full block of ten homes. One day the residents came home to find that bulldozers had leveled the block. Horrified they went to their local government in despair, only to be told they had to provide deeds to show they owned the land, deeds on property their family had lived on for generations. There were no deeds. Ever. They had no money, so could not hire lawyers for a legal fight. Besides, the courts were notoriously corrupt, as was the local government. Our hosts were afraid their block would be next. They had nowhere to go.

Imagine, then, tens of thousands of these young boys and men with a clear analysis that the dire circumstances of their lives are rooted in the interference of this foreign power. Imagine that these boys meet as men and learn they have this in common. How would they not want to avenge the force that dismantled their lives, their families, their security?

You wonder why they hate us? I wonder why they wouldn't. As the Bush administration pitched the folly in Iraq to us under the guise of retaliation, did we ask "How will this impact us in generations to come? Will our approach create more terrorists?"

It has been the policy of our country to manipulate and terrorize people from nations around the world under the codified, racist, patronizing belief that a Euro-centric country knows what's best for brown-skinned people. And where did it get us?

- Anti-U.S. governments in Central and South America
- Terrorist groups in the Philippines
- The Never-Ending War in the Middle East
- 6,717 U.S. military dead in Iraq and Afghanistan
- 50,897 U.S. military wounded in Iraq and Afghanistan
- 22 U.S. military suicides a day (as of Nov. 2013)
- Post-war expansion of Al Qaeda in Iraq

And now we wade into another mess we've created. We broke it, we have to fix it; but is the fix sustainable or yet another smoke-and-mirrors job with consequences for future generations? If you're under 35, you may want to weigh in heavily on this one. You're the ones who'll have to pay the price, the cost of racism writ large.

10. ALL GETTING ALONG

In response to a conversation about the differing role of race in various countries, a young, white acquaintance said, "People just need to get to know one another, spend time with each other, that's all." My response: "Bullshit."

He seemed to believe that if white people and people of color, particularly black people, would just take the time to get to know one another we would all just get along. Here's why I responded with "bullshit."

How many of us does a white person have to get to know? Obviously (anyway I think it's obvious), one wouldn't be enough since we do come in a variety of political, social, religious, ethical, economic, educational and other stripes. So how many black people does a white person have to "get to know" in order to let go of their generalized presumptions about us? And while the challenge is huge in our town, if his theory is true, wouldn't racism have been eliminated in places like Philadelphia, Chicago, New York and Atlanta that have a higher ratio of people of color to whites?

Also, if this were an effective strategy, wouldn't the oppression of women have stopped long ago? The ratio of women to men, even here in geeky Seattle, is low enough that everybody has a fair enough sampling of the genders to "get to know" one another. Yet it's taken decades and we still haven't eradicated education and other barriers that keep women from achieving self-defined lives.

And finally this. Why should my ability to get a job that I'm more than qualified for rely on whether or not a white person has learned to like black people? Either I can do the job, or I can't. Either I know how to write C++ or I don't. Either I know the difference between SQL and MySQL or Java and JavaScript, or I don't. Either I know the tax code and how to apply it, or I don't. Either I can diagnose and repair the problem with your car, or I can't. Either I can retile your roof, or I can't. And once I can do the job, why do I have to rely on whether or not white people like black people in order to feel safe in my workplace?

So let's get down to the real deal, unpack the coded language. What my young, white acquaintance was saying, consciously or not, was, "If you people would just make more of an effort so we can get to know you, all would be well." He presumes that racism is about personal, individual, relationship, which it is not. As my friend the late Rev. Angela Davis used to say, "One of the most diverse places in U.S. history was the plantation." It wasn't the lack of knowledge that marked slavery's oppression. It was the imbalance of power based on heritage and skin color. Racism is an enforced system of policies, practices, and social behaviors that assumes the superiority of all things related to white people. Changing such a system requires more than just liking one another. It requires white people realizing that they are not superior to any other group of people and removing the barriers they've erected to keep others from proving them wrong. And it requires that people of color keep proving them wrong anyway, even with the barriers in place.

This "get to know you" bit is a dodge, and it's embarrassing how many white people use it.

This leads me to the next dodge: "All we need is love." I have several problems with this premise. First, foremost, in a democracy I should be able to get justice whether or not I'm loved. Proving lovability is nowhere stated as a condition in our constitution. And no one ever seems to suggest that white people are the ones who need love before they can find housing, jobs, or justice. It's always people of color.

The shooting of nine people in Emanuel AME Church of Charleston, SC was **NOT ABOUT HATE**. It was about power. This is an important— no, a critical distinction. That white boy didn't want to show how much he hated black people. He wanted to show that he had the power to extinguish our lives with impunity. He wanted to start a race war so that white people could assert and hold on to power. He hated black people because he felt we were stealing his power. It's all about power!

This is the difference between knowing whether too much caffeine, or a tumor causes your headache. If it's a tumor, you can cut down on caffeine all you want and the headache won't go away. THIS is what keeps happening. People want to throw this amorphous thing called love at racism. Oddly, the racism never goes away. That's because the cure doesn't fit the cause.

So, until (1) white people admit that in order to hold on to power they have to give up their empathy and humanity, (2) white people reclaim their empathy and humanity by redefining what power is and how we share it, and (3) people of color claim the full extent of our power by using it or withdrawing it as needed—until then, these incidents will continue. Stop it!

11. WE ARE NOT ALL CREATED EQUAL

The saying used to be "We are all created equal *in the sight of god*." Somehow the last five words have been dropped (which is fine with me), but that leaves an implication that we are all made exactly the same way, and that's not at all true. That distinction is important.

It's even more important because nobody actually believes it. The only time it's invoked is when we talk about race, gender, or sexual orientation. In each instance it's used as coded language to say "People of color are made just like white people" or "Gay people are made just like straight people" or "Women are just like men." In all instances, the oppressor group is used as the standard of measure. Ridiculous.

I have referred in earlier posts to my family's move to Northern California. We were one of a handful of black families in a population of 10,000. I was the second black child to enter their school district. The first was five years older than me and had attended elementary and junior high schools in another town.

Let's set the scene with a bit of information about my educational background. I entered Nazareth School in Addis Ababa when I was four years old. Nazareth was/is a Catholic-run girls' school started with support from the imperial government just the year before I entered. The classes were very large and included girls from every walk of life, regardless of economic status, including girls who lived in traditional mud-and-thatch homes, members of the royal family, and daughters of the elite. I rode to school each day in a limousine with the emperor's grandchildren and returned each evening with my nanny on a mule-drawn, open carriage called a ghari.

Four-year-old girls were supposed to learn needlework: embroidery, basic sewing, needlepoint and the like. I liked those things, but I would frequently sneak out of my classroom and sneak into the class for five year olds, where they were learning the English and Amharic alphabets, basic reading, and numbers. The teachers and my parents eventually figured out what was going on and let me continue the year attending both classes. The next year, I went into first grade. In first grade, we learned more reading, cursive writing, addition, and subtraction. In second grade, we moved on to multiplication, division and fractions (including adding, subtracting, multiplying and dividing them). I left Ethiopia when I was seven, at the end of second grade.

While we were living with my aunt, in Berkeley, I began third grade in a Catholic school. Unlike the kind, patient, loving nuns in Addis, these nuns were cruel. One nun repeatedly hit my knuckles with a ruler because each time she told me to write my name, I did it in cursive. I had never learned block printing, but she assumed that I was being "a show off" and defiant. Each time she'd ask, I'd try to do it better and she'd hit me harder. It was the first time in my life I'd ever been hit by an adult. It took intervention by my mother to clarify the error the nun was making.

When we moved to the suburbs, my parents tried to get me transferred into the local Catholic school, but they wouldn't accept "my kind." So, public school it was. This was supposed to be a good thing because the school district was considered one of the best in the state. But. The school district required that I take an IQ test before I could enroll in their schools. So, I did.

I scored the highest IQ their district had ever recorded. Of course, I had to take it a second time. The numbers stood. Did the district celebrate the fact that they had a "genius" in their midst? Ha! Not a chance. They were embarrassed. This little black girl from Africa had outscored thousands of white children throughout the history of their district. Oops. The joke, of course, was that I'd just left a classroom full of little girls just like me in an Ethiopian classroom who could probably out-perform me in a heartbeat. Among them, I was only one of many, many equals. What the California suburb's school district labeled as genius was actually the average product of very good education.

There were adult conversations about skipping me three grades and putting me in sixth grade. My naïve parents decided it would be "better for my socialization" if I stayed in third grade.

Being hated every day is a wearing experience. My little eight-year-old brain (genius does not equal wisdom) decided that since I couldn't do anything about the race thing or the female thing, I would do something about the genius thing. The result: I began to tutor other students, who would get As, and then I would intentionally get Cs. Where I could, I dumbed myself down as much as possible to remove at least that target from my back. In sixth grade, when a new, white girl beat my IQ, she was celebrated and hailed as the pride of our town.

From this childhood experience, I learned that **white people can't stand for a person of color, especially a black person, to be better than they are**. In fact, I learned it was dangerous for a person of color to reveal how much better they are than any given white person. When white people say that all people are created equal, they are actually saying "You might be equal, but you can't ever be better than I am." That's why people like the Williams sisters get death threats; why white people took such delight in Tiger Woods' demise; and why, ladies and gents, we are seeing this spate of black celebrities with problems being highlighted in the news. It's why Seattle media shows us the flaws in one black leader after another but hides the decades of alcoholism, kleptomania, drug use, domestic violence, and sexual abuse among whites in leadership.

I used to think this dumbing-down survival strategy was unique to me. Then one day I was visiting with a black acquaintance that lives in a beautiful home overlooking Lake Washington. We were talking about Seattle's passive racism as we were looking at the view. She laughed and told me that she had only invited a few white people into her home. She had noticed that those who visited always expressed surprise at how nice her home was and then, after their visit, acted very differently around her. She noticed a competitiveness and meanness that consistently arose.

We are not all created equal. I'm a terrible visual artist and will easily and readily admit that Sharon Arnold, Jazz Brown or George Jennings are superior to me in that realm. I will easily give Omar Willey, Inye Wokoma, or Marc Hoffman kudos for being photographers at a level better than I will ever attain in this lifetime. Jose Amador, Jennifer Jasper or Bob Flor write plays at a level far above my paltry attempts. And don't ever ask me to act! But I'm a damned good essayist and poet. I sing really well. I'm a superb public speaker and trainer. And I have a mind that does amazing and wonderful things that other people's minds can't even begin to do. Sometimes, what I do is better, much better, than what most white people do. Sometimes, like Venus and Serena Williams, I'm even the best.

"Equality" is a lovely, vague, term that's easy to hang as a goalpost because it's immeasurable. It's a dodge. There are ways that I am superior to individual white people. The day I can say that without repercussion, the day the majority of white people can live with that without trying to prove me somehow flawed and inferior, I will believe racism is dead.

12. YOU ARE NOT NORMAL

Some of you are saying to yourselves "and what's normal, there's no such thing." I'll address that later. First, a story.

Story #1:

A while back I attended a piano recital of five Seattle pianists playing the music of Hungarian composer Béla Bartók. They played pieces written by Bartók as well as compositions, some their own, based on a Bartók piece or taken from other composers and arranged in a Bartók style. One of the pianists, a young, white, man introduced a piece he was about to play by saying something, "Bartók was the first to use atonality in music."

Huh? Bartók was born in 1881. Was there no atonal music before him? I grew up in the Greek Orthodox Church. In Africa. Atonal music was… wait a minute… wait just a minute. Who decides what is atonal? Atonal infers that something is against the tone. What tone? What is the standard against which tonality is measured?

I set the thought aside so I could just enjoy the music before me, but it kept bugging me. Then, later in the program, another pianist, an Asian-American woman, introduced a piece by explaining that one of her first assignments in composition class was to write a composition based on an ancient Egyptian chord. She played the chord and then the piece.

Ah, it all came together then. When the young pianist said "first to use atonality in music," he meant in Western European music. What he was citing as atonal has existed in Eastern Europe, Asia, South Asia, and Africa for millennia. In fact, in many of those cultures, the twelve-tone scale used in Western European music might be considered atonal.

So back to the question of what constitutes atonality versus tonality. Who decides what makes a tone tonal? Here's what our friends at Wikipedia have to say about this:

> More narrowly, the term *atonality* describes music that does not conform to the system of tonal hierarchies that characterized classical European music between the seventeenth and nineteenth centuries (Lansky, Perle, and Headlam 2001). "The repertory of atonal music is characterized by the occurrence of pitches in novel combinations, as well as by the occurrence of familiar pitch combinations in unfamiliar environments" (Forte 1977, 1).

More narrowly still, the term is sometimes used to describe music that is neither tonal nor serial, especially the pre-twelve-tone music of the Second Viennese School, principally Alban Berg, Arnold Schoenberg, and Anton Webern (Lansky, Perle, and Headlam 2001). However, "[a]s a categorical label, 'atonal' generally means only that the piece is in the Western tradition and is not 'tonal'" (Rahn 1980, 1), although there are longer periods, e.g., medieval, renaissance, and modern modal musics to which this definition does not apply. "[S]erialism arose partly as a means of organizing more coherently the relations used in the preserial 'free atonal' music. ... Thus many useful and crucial insights about even strictly serial music depend only on such basic atonal theory" (Rahn 1980, 2).

So there it is. Tonal is defined by the classical Western European norm that existed between the 17th and 19th centuries. Atonal is defined as anything that's not that. Western European standards are, once again, held up as the norm that all other things must be gauged against. If it doesn't conform to what's heard as normal in Western European culture, then it's against the tone, i.e. atonal. Two- to three hundred years later, a young man stands on stage and announces to the audience that Béla Bartók invented atonality.

This brings up another, related, subject: language. There's a reason that Italians are overrepresented among opera stars, and it's biological. Well, sort of biological. The tones used in opera are formed by very specific manipulation of the mouth, throat, vocal chords and other parts of the speech mechanism. Those parts can be trained, but for Italians they are an extension of the mechanics already used in their everyday speech. For English-speakers, the mechanical formations needed for opera are not natural, and must be learned. The same is true for country and western singing, which is an outgrowth of regional speech. Classic Chinese opera uses speech mechanics that are challenging to a classic Italian opera singer.

To hold up a single tonal scale as "normal" is to declare the culture that gave it birth as "normal" and all other culture as abnormal. Arabic, Farsi, Chinese, Vietnamese, Cambodian and other Asian cultures, most African cultures, and many Eastern European cultures don't adhere to the 12-note scale that was declared the Western European norm and set as the measure for what is tonal.

This sense of what is "normal" permeates racist culture: style of dance, characters of the alphabet, children's behavior, what is polite/rude, what is corrupt/acceptable, expressions of sexuality/sensuality, food, style of walk, meanings of facial expressions, speech volume, use of color, clothing styles, grammar, and so much more.

Story #2:

My eighth grade graduation dance. *{There really ought to be a mechanism for erasing some memories... perhaps in Humans 2.0.}* Everyone knew this was a big deal. After graduation I was going to be in **high school!** At 13, having skipped a grade, I was the youngest in my class. My mother, on hearing that the dance was going to require that I wear a fancy dress, proceeded to take my measurements, design and make me a beautiful dress. A beautiful, gold brocade, form-fitted, cocktail dress. Very 21st Century, but very out of place among the 1963, pink, yellow, and blue pastel chiffon dresses worn over layers of petticoats by every other girl at the dance. *{Do young women today even <u>know</u> what a petticoat is? I do hope not.}*

My mother's lifelong normal definition of a fancy dress never included chiffon or taffeta. Her norm included fabrics like silk, satin, brocades, or velvet. Marginalized from U.S. culture, she had no idea what the norm was. Excluded from my school's social culture, I had no clue either. Not until I walked into my eighth grade graduation dance and felt the disapproving stares of adults and fellow-students did I realize how out of synch I was.

Story #3:

In August 2015, a group of black women from the *Sistahs on the Reading Edge Book Club*, including **an 83-year-old woman**, were forced off of the Napa Wine Country train and into police custody because they were too loud (http://thegrio.com/2015/08/24/black-women-humiliated-thrown-off-napa-wine-tour/). The action came after a white woman repeatedly complained that the women were disrupting her enjoyment. At one point she allegedly told them "This isn't a bar," even though the wine train is, in fact, a rolling wine bar. The white woman was gauging their behavior by her standard of what was appropriate and "normal" in a setting like that. I've seen white women respond the same way at an outdoor concert when women of color sang or danced along with the music. The white women sit facing the stage with unexpressive faces until a person of color verbally expresses joy or moves their body in response to the music. Then the white woman turns to glower at the person of color. What makes the story of the Napa Wine Country train racist is the response of the institution and the police. One white woman complains and institutions move to make her comfortable and ensure she "feels safe," regardless of whether or not her safety has, in actuality, been threatened.

So back to the original question: What is "normal?" The answer is that normal is a subjective term influenced by the context of time and place. Yet decisions are made every day based on what one considers normal. The person charged with casting for a play might believe that a family consists of a white man, his white wife, and their two white children and may go about casting the play that way. In Seattle, though, there are a very large number of trans-racial families, many of whom are led by gay/lesbian parents. Some of those families are ethnically mixed biologically; others, through adoption. And if one's own family isn't ethnically mixed, one's friends' families are. So, in Seattle, that casting director would be incorrect in their assumptions about what constitutes family.

In the workplace, there are often assumptions about what constitutes normal behavior. Smiling is one of those culturally specific behaviors that are often required of women. Many cultures view constant smiling as a sign of mental illness and reserve a smile for actually humorous moments.

I could write for days about this, but will end with this: Stop thinking European-based culture is normal, it isn't. If someone is behaving in ways outside of your "norm," and you're feeling uncomfortable, ask yourself if that discomfort is something the other person intended, or is it simply a reflection of your own cultural limitation? Check yourself in the work place, in organizations you might belong to, and at any educational institution you touch. How many places in your life do you assume you're normal and get irritated with those who aren't?

When this normative presumption becomes racism is when law, policy or social pressure enforces it. Demanding that everyone in the United States speak only English is racist. Funding only artists who paint using Western European standards and techniques, or musicians who compose classical European music is racist. Showcasing only poets of color who specialize in spoken word, without including those who practice a range of other poetry, is racist.

Question your own normalcy before questioning anyone else, especially before requiring the power of the law behind it.

13. Right and Wrong

As a recent panel discussion about racism and the local arts scene, a panelist said (paraphrase): "There are no right answers. We each have opinions and at some point we will all be uncomfortable. But there are no right answers here tonight." Had curiosity about the outcome of the evening not weighed me down, I would have walked out at that very minute, recognizing it for what it was to prove itself to be: an attempt to mollify everyone; oppressed AND oppressor, yet another "y'all be polite while we hold a gun to your head" event.

There ARE right answers, and wrong. For example, these statements are all true:

- The world is round.
- Apples fall to the earth.
- There really are electrons, protons, and neutrons whizzing all around, through, and in us.
- Humans, as we know them, came from the mountains of Ethiopia.
- Murder is bad.
- Rape is bad.
- And this: our DNA proves we are one species with varied adaptations to meet the natural environment we exist in.

These statements are false:

- The world is flat
- Apples fall to the sky
- Horses and birds can mate
- There are green men on Mars and the moon is made of cheese
- Stealing is bad.

Whenever we come upon a subject that's difficult to discuss, there are those who want to make everyone feel safe before the conversation can happen. I'm not in that camp. I want people to know that racism (the presumption that white people are superior and all the systems in place which support that lie) is evil. Bad. Wrong.

If you believe it's okay to make money using cartoonish caricatures of Native Americans' while they are telling you it's not OK, then you are a racist because you've decided your judgment of what is right trumps theirs. That is bad. Wrong answer. Evil.

If you believe it's okay to make money by using makeup to turn yourself into a caricature of someone from another culture, you're wrong. That is bad. Evil. Even if you're *not* making any money from doing it, it's wrong.

If you believe it's okay to write stories about people whose culture you know nothing about, as if it was your culture, you're wrong. That is bad. Evil.

Get the drift? There *are* right answers, and they are founded on respect and accountability. If your opinion is based on anything else, it's the wrong answer. Period. If you have to be made "comfortable" and "safe" before you can discuss racism, then you are a racist because you are demanding that people of color remain uncomfortable and unsafe until your needs are met. You are demanding that the world revolve around your needs. That's racist.

14. CAN'T WE ALL JUST GET ALONG?

My friend was a stunningly beautiful woman. Nearly six feet tall, with shoulder-length white hair, steel-gray eyes, and unlined, porcelain skin, she was a striking woman who instantly drew attention when she entered a room. She had been an activist for many years, a champion for women's equal pay and access to health care. She marched against U.S. aggression in Central America and was a passionate defender of civil rights, including gay rights. Now in her 50s, she had become a mentor to a new generation of white, female activists.

She came by these positions honestly. As a survivor of childhood sexual trauma and two violently abusive marriages she understood oppression from the inside. We were good friends working on the same side of many causes and rooted in a similar spiritual quest.

One night, after a particularly challenging meeting, we were walking down the street toward our cars. In the dim light of a streetlamp we could see a tall, handsome man dressed in khakis and a light jacket walking toward us. I started to smile and nod, as is the custom between African Americans in most cities. I was startled when my friend suddenly gripped my arm tightly and froze. I looked up to see absolute terror in her eyes. I asked what was wrong. By this time the man had walked passed us and was well on his way down the street. I asked if she knew the man. She didn't. Realizing the answer, I asked what made her so afraid. "Oh," she replied, "I just wasn't sure what… you can't be too careful."

A few weeks later she and I took a road trip to a conference in Milwaukee. Neither of us had been to there before. We had a great time on the two-day drive; talking about the upcoming conference, discussing situations back home, listening to music.

We arrived in the city late at night. I was driving, and a bit tired. She was navigating, something she didn't do well. She told me to take an exit from the freeway, and we were very soon lost. We were driving on a four-lane boulevard. Bars, restaurants, bus stops, and small shops lined both sides.

I've loved road trips since I was a child travelling the mountain roads of Ethiopia with my father, and reading the map of a new city is one of the tangential joys. After about fifteen minutes, I suggested I pull the car over and look at the map. She responded with, "not in this neighborhood!" I looked around. The neighborhood looked fine to me. It was well lit, there were a few people walking by and a few more at a nearby bus stop. There was a mom-and-pop grocery and gas station down the road. It looked pretty much like the neighborhood we had left back home.

Then it hit me. Every person I saw was black. I asked if she knew the neighborhood, had been there before and knew it to be unsafe. No, she hadn't, and didn't. Too tired to go any deeper, I took the map and found the way to our hotel. Though our relationship continued to be collegial, I slowly disengaged from our friendship.

A white man had raped this woman in her childhood. White husbands had physically and emotionally abused her. White men had cheated her financially. White men had withheld power from her professionally. Where did she direct her fear? Towards black people, who had never harmed her or anyone she knew.

I was reminded of these stories in the past few months. When **#BlackLivesMatter** took over Bernie Sanders speech at Westlake Center in Seattle, many of my black friends were traumatized by the reactions of their white friends, people they saw as more than allies, more than colleagues. Few had been in circumstances where those relationships were tested by action versus talk. And they were in abject grief.

From these experiences, and way too many more like them, I've learned that "Can't we all just get along?" really means "Can't you just shut up and make me feel safe?" White people, especially white women, don't seem to want to make any *effort* to get along. They don't want to examine their own irrational fears and behaviors. They just want black people, and people of color in general, to just stop making them uncomfortable.

With their lenses focused on the scary black people, they miss the John Wayne Gacys, Josh Powells, and Bernie Madoffs in their midst.

15. How Numbers Lie to Save White People

It's a gathering of progressives at a private home overlooking Elliott Bay. The potluck is over and the thirty or so attendees, all but two of whom are white, are gathered around the living and dining rooms. A woman is giving a presentation about the county's new program to provide more effective preschool for children of color. She says it's the most effective way to intervene in their education and then explains that, since statistics show that children of color are more likely to be disciplined than white children, the program will provide a psychologist to help the teacher deal with emerging issues. It isn't until I point out that the discipline issues have been shown to be a result of teacher bias and that she's left out the key words "more likely to be disciplined *for the same infraction*" that she mentions that the psychologists are there to help the teachers deal with *their* bias, and not to fix the children.

At a major Pacific Science Center exhibit about the impact of racism in the Northwest, the walls are lined with posters that proclaim that African Americans have the lowest high school graduation rates, the lowest test scores in reading, math and science, the highest drop-out rates, the highest unemployment rates, the highest incarceration rates, and on and on. To the casual observer, and most people are casual observers, this is proof that black people are lazy, slow, uninterested in education, untrustworthy, criminal. In each case, the information is only partially presented and highly misleading.

The statistics presented don't include how a child's learning is impacted by their parent's inability to find work. They don't show how a white, female teacher's fear of black men is manifested in her reaction to a joyful, naturally ebullient, extrovert in the body of a five-year-old black boy. They don't reflect the multi-generational impact of substandard buildings, textbooks, and equipment. They don't reveal the exhausting stories that parents of color tell of fighting in one system to save their child's life, only to have it attacked by another system. They don't divulge the staggering difference between which racial categories actually commit the most crime and which are jailed.

The people who create these statistics know the backstories. So why aren't they giving the entire picture to the public? The answer is embarrassingly simple. Parents of color are facing discriminatory employment and housing practices that give whites preferential treatment. White men and women (mostly women) make up the majority of teachers and administrators in US public schools. White men commit the majority of crime in almost every town and city in the US, yet receive less punishment.

To tell the truth about these statistics would mean putting the responsibility for behavioral, political, social, and cultural change on white people. It would remind white people that these systems were put in place to benefit them while causing intentional, ongoing, damage to people and communities of color.

To continue to tell these half-truths is a delusion white people cannot afford. Your children may not be going to jail, but they continue to become criminals on Main Street and on Wall Street. As the Romans, Nazis, Fascists and other delusional societies would tell you, it's unsustainable. It's just a matter of time.